3 LIFE HACKS TO SUCCESS

JONATHON P HIBBARD

3 LIFE HACKS TO SUCCESS

JONATHON P HIBBARD

TABLE OF CONTENTS

3 Life Hacks to Success

I am so glad you decided to read this book. You must be someone with tremendous potential waiting to be unlocked. You have been working and grinding throughout the years, improving every day. Most people do not understand the struggle and effort it takes to reach the top. You have tasted success in small doses and are ready for more. You have the work ethic but want your freedom. Freedom to enjoy your family and friends and to live the life you were destined to achieve. That is why I am so glad you are reading this book. This short book will help you unlock simple hacks to succeed in business and life and unlock the key to your freedom.

We are all working toward something; if not defined by you, the life you want to live will slip through your fingers. I started my career without a defined goal of what I truly wanted to become. I have been a teacher, insurance agent, call center representative, delivery boy, painter, and anything else I could to make ends meet. It wasn't until I defined who I wanted to become things changed for me. I discovered that life gives you cheat codes along the way, but you have to play the game to unlock the codes. Most people never play the game; they watch from the sidelines and complain that others' success was by luck. That is not who you are; you have played for a long time. You are ready to level up; you put in the hard work and still feel stuck at the same level for years. You can not figure out how to beat the cycle. You have tried and failed through the years. You work hard and are passionate but have not unlocked the three simple hacks to help you finish the game.

Great news: you are about to level up and win at every game in life you play going forward.

LEVEL 1 - VISION

"Success in life is what you do with your ideas and vision. While action is important, the first step of success deals with training your mind." —Matthew Toren, author, entrepreneur, and investor

I remember one of the first video games I ever played, Super Mario Brothers from Nintendo. Suppose you have never played it. It's super simple. Mario, the main character, has a starting point and has to defeat enemies on each level until he reaches a castle at the end of the level. Each time you conquer a level, you can advance to other worlds to eventually defeat the main boss, a turtle named Bowser, who has stolen the Princess Peach. Mario's goal is to save the Princess. Each level he conquers, he is disappointed to see that the Princess is not there, and he has to continue his quest.

We can learn much from Mario and his quest; Mario knows his goals. Mario has a clear vision of what he is trying to accomplish. His job is to save his Princess, but nothing will stop him from reaching that goal. The cool part is that you control Mario's outcome. He can only advance if you allow him to. He is on a mission to save the Princess.

The first hack to level up your life is vision. I have lacked vision throughout my life, and when I did, I paid the price for it. I wasted years at dead-end jobs just hoping for my big break. When it never came, I would get frustrated like I was Mario, never finishing the level, just walking around and not advancing to the next world. You may be in the same position I was in; you work hard but can not determine why you are stuck.

My lightbulb moment came to me when I was working at a call center, taking angry phone calls from people who did not want to call me. I was talking to a friend who mentioned becoming a manager at this call center and implied that I should apply, too. At that moment, I thought the pay would be a lot more. But then it hit me: why in the hell am I here? How did I get to this point where I was sitting in a call center and getting yelled at by strangers? Why would I allow myself to get stuck on this level? I had to look hard at myself and realize it was all my fault.

I grew up in a small town in Southeastern Kentucky; if you know anything about Southeastern Kentucky, we have horses, bourbon, and no jobs. I grew up in a small trailer; my parents dropped out of high school, my dad worked at a factory, and my mom was a waitress. We did not have much, but they loved us and worked hard. The mindset in my region was to get a job and work until you retired— no big goals or dreams. Just do what you have to survive. But I knew there was something different about myself growing up; I was a dreamer. I wanted to do more than my peers, and I wanted to be better than the average. I was not sure what that looked like, but I wanted more.

So when the moment hit me that I settled for the call center position, it hit me hard. I immediately gave my two weeks' notice without the prospect of a new job. It was not the smartest thing I have done, but it changed my destiny forever. I realized that I had no vision and no goals for myself. The dreams of my youth faded, and I was stuck, and I wanted out. I wanted to complete the level and move on to the next world.

Before I walked into the unemployment office, looking for a job a few weeks later, I had done one thing I had never done before. I wrote down what I wanted my life to look like ten years from now. I wanted to make sure that the path I took going forward would help me reach my goals, and if it did not fit into achieving my goals, then it was not for me.

That is the hack to level one; it's writing down where you want to be 1, 5, or 10 years from now.

You can not start the game without knowing where you end up. Every game you play has an ending, but most people drift along in life and never define how they will get to the end. It sounds simple, and it is. You have to document what you want your life to look like in the future. You have to see in your mind where you will end up. Just like Mario knew he would save Princess Peach. Without vision, you will not succeed.

Why are you stuck? You are a talented, hard-working person, but you have not sat down and documented where you want your life to be ten years from now. Why is this so important? Your mind is potent, but it can be easily manipulated into taking the path of least resistance. It's easier to stay the course and be safe. Your mind loves safety, but success does not. Success comes to those who take the risk. Mario would not have been able to save the Princess if he'd stayed at level 1, but he had to fight bad guys to get to her. He had to risk his life to reach the goal. Your mind wants to avoid taking risks. Before you can start level one, you need to define the goal before your mind allows you to take the risk to move forward.

I love 10-year goals; I love to think long-term and then set smaller goals to help me reach the longer ones. I was able to hit every one of my 10-year goals after I quit my call center job. It was difficult, and I had plenty of failures, but I never gave up. Mario gets killed along the way but has extra lives; when we get knocked down, we must get back up and keep trying. If you do not move forward, you will not grow. I know some of you may be asking yourself, that's it. Writing down my goals seems too simple. This is the first life hack to success. It is simple, but most people never do it. Lack of documentation will lead to a lack of persistence in life, and where you are not persistent, you will fail. Failure, to me, is not about getting knocked down or humbled; failure is never trying in the first place.

You can not move forward if you do not know where you are going. Do you take a trip and not look up directions? Do you drive randomly in your car, praying that you reach your destination? That is ridiculous; you first document your destination, and then you can map out how you will get there. It's the same in life. You have to write down where you want to go and then break it down into smaller goals to help you reach your destination.

Level one hack to success is simple: document where you want to be ten years from now. Be like Mario, know what you want to accomplish, and do not stop until you reach it. You control your life, and just as you control Mario, it's up to you if you reach the end of the game.

LEVEL 2 - EXECUTION

"Quality is never an accident; it is always the result of high intention, sincere effort, intelligent direction, and skillful execution; it represents the wise choice of many alternatives."
—William A. Foster, World War II era Medal of Honor awardee

Lack of execution is like wanting to win the lottery without buying a ticket. You have to play the game to have a chance at winning. Before you win the lottery, you first need to acquire two dollars, then drive yourself to the local lottery store and purchase a ticket. They don't hand out millions to people wishing to win. It would be nice to document all of your goals, and then magically, they all fall into place, and your life is incredible. Life hack number two is about executing a proven documented process that will allow you to reach your goals.

You are a hard worker, but are you a competent worker? I had an employee who always worked as hard as possible and went above and beyond for me. I thought she was terrific; I would brag to others about how hard she worked for me. After she left my office, I hired someone with 17 years of experience, and she showed me that working hard does not necessarily mean working more efficiently. She would accomplish the tasks in half the time my previous worker took. She did more in a few hours than the previous employee did all day. Her years of experience taught her how to execute effectively, and she developed standard operating procedures over time, allowing her to be more efficient.

When I was a kid, I would get so upset when Mario would get killed in the game, but over time, I developed new skills that allowed me to control that little digital dude to beat the game. When you start to work on your dreams and goals, you will encounter many difficult situations and fail. Don't be discouraged; failure is part of the process. It's an opportunity to learn from your mistakes and develop methods and procedures to ensure you become as efficient as possible.

This life hack takes some time before it's perfected. Businesses with success have operating procedures to ensure that they run at a high level and can replicate the process daily. If your goals have you starting or running a business, then you need to study every successful person in your field and ask a few of them about their standard operating procedures for their business. Processes lead to execution.

For example, what steps do you take to contact a client if you miss their call? As simple as this may sound, you will be surprised how many clients I acquire each year because my competitors never call their clients back. This can also apply to your life; what steps will you take daily to help you reach your goals? If your 10-year goals include losing weight, what are you doing daily to help you achieve that goal? If your goal is to run your own company, what are you doing to prepare yourself today and every day going forward? You need to have a document that you have typed up on what steps and procedures you need to do so that you are consistent and persistent at reaching your goals.

Lack of persistence may be the reason you have failed in the past. Lack of documentation is why you lack persistence. You have no accountability, nothing to challenge your effort against. After documenting the end goal, you must break it down into small everyday steps to help you achieve it. It will take time and can be time-consuming, but if those other offices had a procedure to follow up with clients who called, I would not have taken their business away from them. I have procedures for every step in my office, from when someone walks in the door until they leave. I have been guilty of not following my guidelines, and that's when I started to go backward in my business. I have updated and modified my procedures throughout the years. It's a living document that can adjusted throughout life.

To have more freedom, you need to be able to track your execution to make sure you are hitting your targets. Something to consider is finding someone with interests similar to yours and having them as your accountability partner. Share your goals and procedures with them, and meet with them once a month to challenge you when you fall short. Then, have them reward you when you hit your goals. Having someone to challenge you will only make you better and reach success faster.

I am now a very successful financial advisor for one of the biggest firms in the United States. Fifteen years ago, I was delivering packages for a printing company. I got to where I am today because of my vision for the future and my execution. I am by no way perfect. I have so many things I still want to accomplish, but I was laser-focused on reaching my goals, and it was my execution of the details that allowed me to succeed faster than my competition.

If you want to be faster at reaching your goals, focus on the execution. In sports, athletes have the vision to win the championship game, but their attention to the small details is how they reach the big game. They master executing the small goals daily to help them improve their craft. You have to think this way to become the best you can be. Executing a proven process will allow you to become efficient and reach your goals faster. Learn to be the best in your field; this will bring you the freedom you deserve.

Like Mario, you must execute or play the game to make it to the end. If you want to own your business, create a business plan for your future business. If you're going to become CEO of your company, document how you would run the company and the steps you will take every day to help you get to that position, for example, going back to school to earn a master's degree. Documented processes help you execute your vision faster.

If you want to win the lottery, you have to buy the ticket.

LEVEL 3 - RELATIONSHIPS

"We're a team. It's part of our job to help each other out and to forgive each other quickly. Otherwise, we'd never get anything done." —Jeramey Kraatz

Even though Mario has Luigi, life is too hard to do it alone. Looking back over two decades of my career, I would not be where I am today without the relationships I have built. It's all about becoming a lone wolf in today's society. Taking on the world all by yourself and always looking out for your best interest are the norms of American culture. I am all for becoming the best version of yourself; that's how you grow and become more efficient. But I can't entirely agree with the lone wolf mindset that you don't need anyone else to help you reach the top. Most of this thinking today can be derived from hurt people who no longer trust others. The truth is hurt people who decide to live alone will never find peace. They may seem successful on the outside, but deep down, they can not find joy until they learn to forgive those who offended them.

This brings me to hack number three: forgiveness. To be in any successful relationship, you must learn to master forgiveness. There will be managers, clients, spouses, and many friends who will offend and hurt you at some point in your life. People are messy, and relationships are complicated. That is why it's easier to become a lone wolf, but it's selfish, too. You never know when that one friendship or relationship will become the key to unlocking your success.

I would not be a financial advisor today without the relationships I built; I would not have been offered the position of financial advisor if I had not cultivated relationships throughout my career. I would not have been able to develop my practice to its success today without the friendships I have made. Think about the relationships you have today; most of us have one or two close friends and a lot of people who think highly of you or badly. Trust takes a long time to build in my line of work and is easy to lose. Reputation is everything, so I try my best to honor my word. When I mess up, I own it and fix it. If I say I will do something, I will do it no matter the cost. I do this because I understand I can not do life alone. I need people to help me professionally and personally. I know without people, I have no influence; I can not make an impact and help make the world a better place. It's not easy, but if you master forgiveness, you can have more relationships to help you later in life.

Forgiveness does not mean you stay best friends with everyone you meet. It means you can let things go and continue to work with others different from you. People who always have to be correct and never forgive will end up alone and bitter, and nobody wants to help the angry, bitter person succeed. Think about it: who would you instead help, someone who is super friendly to you or the angry jerk? This is why it's so necessary never to burn a bridge and learn to forgive others no matter what act they have done to you. Forgiveness is not a reason to stay in a bad relationship, but forgiving others prevents things from bothering you. You can learn to let things roll off your back like water to a duck's back.

This will allow you to build more relationships, and when the time comes, those people can help you move to the next level in your career. You may need them to help you get the promotion; you may need to sell to them or have them refer you to others. You will need people to help you, so you need to get better at helping them first.

People are not the enemy; time is your enemy. When you waste energy on things that do not matter a year from now, you waste time—the time you could use to help others and enjoy your life. Bitterness and poor relationships cause worry and waste years of your life. Like Mario, he was on a timer on each level to save the Princess. You, too, must learn to move to the next level before time runs out.

I have found that the quickest way to build friendships is to have this forgiveness mindset. If you can forgive anyone for any reason, you can walk in freedom and treat people with kindness and respect, and you begin to listen to people and care about their needs before your own. Relationships are about being there for others and caring about their needs before your own. Mario focused his life on saving the Princess. He put his life on the line to help someone else. Learn to forgive, and you will become successful.

SUMMARY

These three life hacks will allow you to reach new career levels and help you get to them quickly. You are a hard worker and now a more competent worker. Having a vision for your life will change everything. You can not get to where you are going without having the destination mapped out. Then, you will execute your vision with documented processes you can replicate. You will save a lot of time and this will lead to success quickly. Most important of all, you need to master the art of forgiveness so you can be the best at building relationships. Do you want to become a lone wolf, but reach the end and end up alone, is it worth it? If you can incorporate these three life hacks, you will be unstoppable.

Good luck, my friends, and thank you again for reading this book. I know it's going to change your life. Just like Mario, you will defeat your enemy and save the Princess. You are amazing and are going to change the world.

REFERENCES:

Super Mario World: Super Mario Advance 2
Super Mario World TM - Super Mario Advance 2 TM ©
1983 - 2002 Nintendo. TM AND ® ARE TRADEMARKS OF
NINTENDO CO., LTD. © 2002 NINTENDO.

"Success in life is what you do with your ideas and vision.
While action is important, the first step of success deals with
training your mind." —Matthew Toren, author, entrepreneur,
and investor

"Quality is never an accident; it is always the result of high
intention, sincere effort, intelligent direction and skillful
execution; it represents the wise choice of many alternatives."
—William A. Foster, World War II era Medal of Honor
awardee

"We're a team. It's part of our job to help each other out,
and to forgive each other quickly. Otherwise, we'd never get
anything done." —Jeramey Kraatz, author

Excerpt From
The Big Book of Business Quotations
Johnnie L. Roberts
https://books.apple.com/us/book/the-big-book-of-
business-quotations/id1448392244

ABOUT THE AUTHOR

Jonathon is from London, Kentucky, and has been married to his wife for 17 years and has four children. He has a passion to help people thrive and become successful. As a Financial Advisor, he has a passion to help his clients reach their long-term financial goals. He and his wife are big NFL fans.

Made in the USA
Columbia, SC
21 October 2024